REAL LIFE ISSUES

COPING WITH
UNEMPLOYMENT

Mary Colson

Heinemann
LIBRARY

Chicago, Illinois

| H | www.heinemannraintree.com Visit our website to find out more information about Heinemann-Raintree books. | To order: ☎ Phone 888-454-2279 ▭ Visit www.heinemannraintree.com to browse our catalog and order online. |

Edited by Louise Galpine and Laura Knowles
Designed by Richard Parker
Original illustrations © Capstone Global Library
    Ltd 2011
Picture research by Liz Alexander

Originated by Capstone Global Library Ltd
Printed and bound in the United States of America,
    North Mankato, MN

15 14 13 12 11
10 9 8 7 6 5 4 3 2 1

Library of Congress Cataloging-in-Publication Data
Colson, Mary.
    Coping with unemployment / Mary Colson. — 1st ed.
        p. cm. — (Real life issues)
    Includes bibliographical references and index.
    ISBN 978-1-4329-4765-1 (hc)
    1. Unemployment—Life skills guides. I. Title.
    HD5708.C65 2010
    331.13'7—dc22
    2010021049

Acknowledgments
The author and publisher are grateful to the following for permission to reproduce copyright material: © Corbis p. 43; Alamy pp. 9 (© Fredrik Renander), 19 (© Shaun-Finch), 31 (© Asia Images Group Pte Ltd), 29 (© Steve Skjold), 37 (© Jim West), Corbis pp. 4 (© PAUL HANNA/Reuters), 12 (© Andy Rain/epa), 15 (© STAFF/Reuters), 17 (© Benjamin Lowy), 8 (© Andrew Fox), 20 (© Inspirestock), 21 (© Tim Pannell), 30 (© moodboard); Getty Images pp. 11 (Image Source), 23 (Bloomberg), 10 (Mark Edward Atkinson/Blend Images), 33 (John Howard/Lifesize), 35 (Bloomberg); Photolibrary pp. 7 (moodboard), 13 (Mel Longhurst/age footstock), 27 (I Love Images), 32 (Stuart Pearce/age footstock), 34 (Celia Peterson/arabianEye), 39 (Fancy), 38 (Helen Stone); Shutterstock pp. 41 (© Monkey Business Images), 5 (© Monkey Business Images), 25 (© Kablonk).

"Distressed texture" design detail reproduced with permission of iStockphoto/© Diana Walters.

Cover photograph of girl reading newspaper in kitchen reproduced with permission of Corbis/© Blasius Erlinger.

Quotation on page 36 extracted from "The Human Side of Agriculture," Robert J. Fetsch, Ph.D., State Extension Specialist and Professor, Department of Human Development & Family Studies, Colorado State University, Fort Collins, Colorado.

We would like to thank Anne Pezalla for her invaluable help in the preparation of this book.

Every effort has been made to contact copyright holders of material reproduced in this book. Any omissions will be rectified in subsequent printings if notice is given to the publishers.

In order to protect the privacy of individuals, some names in this book have been changed.

CONTENTS

⚠ Stay safe on the Internet!
When you are on the Internet, never give personal details such as your real name, phone number, or address to anyone you have only had contact with online. If you are contacted by anyone who makes you feel uncomfortable or upset, don't reply, tell an adult, and block that person from contacting you again.

Any words appearing in the text in bold, **like this**, are explained in the glossary.

Introduction

Having a job and going to work provides money and security for a family. It also establishes a daily routine that everyone is used to. When parents or caregivers lose their jobs and become unemployed, family life can be turned upside down. Unemployment means having no job, and it can affect every person in a family.

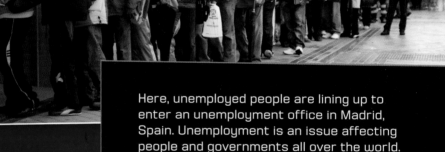

Here, unemployed people are lining up to enter an unemployment office in Madrid, Spain. Unemployment is an issue affecting people and governments all over the world.

Lifestyle changes

Without a job and an **income**, it can be difficult to cope. Some changes to your lifestyle might be necessary. For example, you might not be able to continue with all your usual activities after school and on weekends because they cost too much. Birthday and holiday presents might also be smaller and less expensive. Buying food and paying bills will take **priority** over treats.

If an older brother or sister loses his or her job and has to move back home, family life will also change. Bedrooms might have to be shared. The unemployed person might be emotional and find it difficult to cope. Unemployment can even involve families moving to a new, cheaper home.

How this book can help

This book will explain the reasons why someone might become unemployed, and who might be affected by this change. Most importantly, this book will suggest some ways to help you cope.

Unemployment affects every person in a family, but there are ways to cope.

BEHIND THE HEADLINES

In 2010 the number of unemployed people in the United States was 9.3 million. About 6.3 million of these people had been unemployed for 27 weeks or more.

Why Do People Lose Jobs?

There are many different ways a person can lose a job and become unemployed. A business might close down or move overseas, or it might **restructure**. This means it changes how it organizes and uses its workers, and it might not need as many people. A worker might also become sick and be unable to work. Occasionally, an adult leaves a job for personal reasons, such as wanting a career change or because of family problems. No matter what the reason is, unemployment can be difficult. But how might this affect you?

Routine change

When your parent or caregiver is employed, he or she will be paid regularly. This gives the family money to pay household bills and maybe have some treats, too. You will be used to your parent leaving the house and returning home at certain times. He or she might wear different clothes to go to work, or a uniform. Your family might sometimes have a movie night or a takeout meal as a treat, or go shopping on Saturdays. You might enjoy taking lessons in sports, music, or art. All these things are part of you and your family's routine, but without a job and the security of an **income**, this routine can change.

It isn't easy for a manager to tell people that they are losing their jobs. Phrases like "we're letting you go" try to soften the blow.

How businesses work

When a business has a lot of work, it needs to employ more people. For example, if a factory makes toys that everyone wants, the factory will need more workers to make more toys to keep up with the demand for them. But if the toys become less popular, the factory won't need to make or supply so many. If this happens, the workers will have less work to do, and some may lose their jobs. This is how businesses work. It is called **supply and demand**.

Closing down

If there is no demand for the product a business offers, the business will shut down, and people will become unemployed. For example, when Circuit City closed down, over 30,000 **employees** lost their jobs at over 700 electronics stores. It is difficult to find a new job when so many newly unemployed people are all looking for work at the same time.

Workers will lose their jobs if a store closes down.

The cities of New Delhi and Bangalore are the call center hubs of India.

Going abroad

If your parents have questions about something such as their Internet connection or their bank account, they can call the Internet company or bank for information. However, they might actually be talking on the phone to someone in another country, such as India. Many U.S. businesses have set up **call centers** in India. It costs less to pay a worker in India than it does to pay a worker in the United States, due to the lower **cost of living** there. This in turn means that the service provided by the business costs less for the customer. However, it is estimated that hundreds of thousands of U.S. jobs have been lost in this way.

Unemployment benefits

If your parent loses his or her job, there will not be a paycheck coming in regularly. But that does not mean there will be no money at all for the family to live on. When a person becomes unemployed, there is usually a **payout** from the company called **severance pay**. The amount of money is calculated based on how long the person has worked for the company. In the United States, an unemployed person also receives payments from his or her state government for a certain amount of time. These payments are not the same as a salary, but they help families to pay household bills and buy food.

Counseling

It can be difficult to cope with your parent or caregiver losing his or her job. Talking about your feelings can help. School **counselors** are there to listen and to support you. It is also important to talk to friends about how you are feeling.

Many schools have counselors whom you can talk to in private.

BEHIND THE HEADLINES

In the United States, losing a job means that health insurance is also lost, as it is often provided by employers. If anyone in the family becomes sick, there may no longer be medical insurance to cover the cost of expensive hospital treatment. However, a U.S. government program called COBRA helps unemployed people keep their health insurance for a time after their jobs end.

Some people can't work because of illness or disability. Money from the government helps families to cope.

Why are the jobs in your own country affected by what happens in other countries? What are the major reasons for job losses? How can international issues affect your family?

All connected

We live in a **global economy** in which banking and business are linked together. A problem in one country often affects others. In 2007 a **financial crisis** that began in the United States had far-reaching effects for workers and their families all over the world. It became known as the "credit crunch." People lost their homes because they could not keep up with **mortgage** payments, and thousands of businesses shut down. But what exactly is the credit crunch?

When the credit crunch hit, some banks were forced to close. The banks' workers were among the many people who suddenly lost their jobs.

BEHIND THE HEADLINES

For businesses to grow, they sometimes need to borrow money (also called "credit") from banks and pay it back later. The credit crunch of 2007–2009 happened because banks had lent too much money to people and businesses that could not pay it back. There was a dramatic cash, or credit, shortage. Banks stopped lending, and businesses came to a standstill or even collapsed. This caused massive job losses.

This memorial in Washington, D.C., shows people waiting for **food aid**. During the Great Depression, government support was given out to help people cope.

CASE STUDY

In the 1930s, a long period of **economic** decline called the Great Depression left millions of people around the world unemployed and struggling to cope. Eventually the global economy recovered, and people found new jobs. Depressions do happen sometimes, but they do not last forever.

An industrial process

Machines can be more **efficient** and cheaper than using human workers. They don't get tired or make mistakes, and they don't need to be paid. For over 200 years, engines and machines have been replacing workers in factory and **manufacturing** work. This process is called **industrialization**, and it usually means that jobs are lost. Today, it is not only machines that are replacing workers, but computers, too. The clothing, electronics, and car industries are just some of the areas where unemployment is rising because of new computers.

Fragile China

The Guangdong province of China used to employ thousands of workers in dozens of factories to make toys, plastic goods, and electronics. Many of the toys were **exported** to supply stores in North America and Europe. Now the demand is less because of the global **recession**. Many of the Guangdong factories have closed, leaving thousands of workers unemployed and facing a struggle to feed their families.

BEHIND THE HEADLINES

Industrialization has also affected farming. Machines now harvest crops quicker than workers can, and there are fewer jobs for farmworkers. Because of this, all over China farmworkers left their homes and families in the country to go to the cities for work. They hoped to find jobs in the factories and earn more money. However, the credit crunch of 2007–2009 caused over 70,000 Chinese factories to shut down. This left 20 million **migrant workers** without jobs.

These migrant workers have arrived in the city to look for factory work. Many struggle to find a job.

You can't control the weather

Farming is an occupation that depends on the right weather at the right time. Farmers all over the world have to cope with **unpredictable** weather patterns and even more extreme natural disasters, such as fires, floods, or droughts. Government money and aid are available to cope with the immediate aftereffects of crop failure, but in the long-term, finding a new job outside farming can be difficult.

BEHIND THE HEADLINES

California has a large farming industry and employs thousands of **seasonal** farmworkers during harvest times. A recent three-year-long drought has resulted in failed crops and smaller harvests. Many workers have become unemployed because there is less work to do. The water shortage is being blamed for the loss of around 65,000 jobs.

Hurricane Katrina, job destroyer

In 2005 Hurricane Katrina destroyed much of New Orleans, Louisiana. Properties, businesses, and roads were all so badly damaged or destroyed that workers and their families had to move elsewhere. Offshore oil and gas **refineries** were badly affected, and so were the tourism and fishing industries. This resulted in an estimated 230,000 lost jobs. The state government organized **job fairs** to try to get people back to work, and by the fall of 2006, most people had found new jobs. However, in 2010, just as the region was starting to recover, jobs were once again under threat. This time it was because of the oil spill in the Gulf of Mexico, the worst environmental disaster in U.S. history.

These seasonal farmworkers have been employed by a farm in California. Government food aid is given out in California to help people to cope when they do not have jobs.

The People Behind the Numbers

The main aim of a business is to make money. When business leaders decide they need to save extra money, their **priority** is not always the individual lives that are affected by these decisions. Unemployment affects people from all backgrounds, in all jobs, and in all countries. So, who are the people who have been hit by the **recession**, and what happens when an entire community loses its jobs?

CASE STUDY

In 2009 Max's father, Phil, lost his job in the construction industry. Max remembers Phil coming home and telling the family his news. "He said that the whole site was closing down so there were lots of other people affected. He said the site might open up again when the **economy** improved. He told us not to worry, but we'd all have to try hard to save money."

Children of the unemployed

In 2010 one in seven U.S. children had an unemployed parent. That is 10.5 million children. The credit crunch has been a major contributor to this. Industries most at risk of unemployment are construction, hotels, transportation, banking, and insurance. This is because when people are trying to save, they travel less and spend less money on housing and vacations.

Having unemployed parents can mean there is not much money to pay for activities. It is easy to become bored and think you have nothing to do.

Banking on a job

Traditionally, jobs in banking have been stable and secure. But today, people who work in banks are just as likely as builders and factory workers to lose their jobs. In fact, banks were among the first to suffer job losses during the credit crunch.

BEHIND THE HEADLINES

In 2008 the U.S. bank Lehman Brothers collapsed. This resulted in 45,000 job losses worldwide. The bank failed because it had lent too much money to people who could not afford to pay the money back. Other banks collapsed, too, causing further job losses. Behind every job loss is a person with bills to pay and maybe a family to support.

Thousands of banking jobs were lost in the United States during the credit crunch.

Staying ahead of the competition

When many unemployed people are all looking for a new job at the same time, the competition is very high. Hundreds of people might be pursuing only a few jobs within a certain industry or town. The more contacts and networks an unemployed person has, the better.

Use your computer skills to help your parent search for a job or use a networking site.

Online!

Some professional people use **social networking sites** to help them find a job. These sites work on the basis that it is not what you know, but who you know, and they connect you to many different people. These new contacts might be looking to employ someone who has your family member's skills.

Chain reaction

In many parts of the world, towns develop in support of a single business or main factory, such as car **manufacturing**. In Japan's Toyota City, the main car factory provides the majority of jobs for the 420,000 residents. Other, smaller businesses support the factory. One-industry towns are at risk of high unemployment if the main industry fails. If this happens, it can take years for the town to develop new jobs and recover.

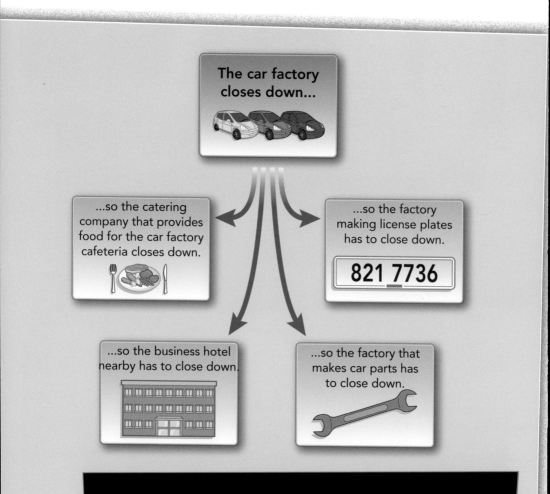

The car factory closes down...

...so the catering company that provides food for the car factory cafeteria closes down.

...so the factory making license plates has to close down.

821 7736

...so the business hotel nearby has to close down.

...so the factory that makes car parts has to close down.

In one-industry towns such as Toyota City, all the businesses in the town depend on each other. This means if one fails, they all suffer. Most of Toyota City's workers are connected to the car plant in some way.

Sometimes a community can work together to make a difference for everyone. Sometimes industries going out of business are in such bad financial shape that they do not want to pay out full **severance pay** to workers. However, there have been instances when workers have **protested** and gotten their severance money paid. Still, these workers face the challenge of finding new jobs.

BEHIND THE HEADLINES

Detroit, Michigan, is known as Motor City. Since the early 1900s, the car industry there has employed many thousands of people. But many car factories have recently shut down because of the credit crunch and less demand for large cars. In 2010 half of all workers in Detroit were unemployed. Today, car companies are developing smaller, cheaper, eco-friendly cars. If these succeed, there could be car factory jobs in Detroit again.

When communities gather together to protest, it is a powerful way of making their feelings clear.

SAVE MY DADDY'S JOB!! NUMII

It is very stressful when someone in your family loses his or her job. Lots of families experience unemployment, and they develop strategies or plans to help them cope. How can unemployment affect life at home?

Sharing with siblings

If an older brother or sister becomes unemployed, he or she may move back into the family home in order to save money while looking for another job. You may even have to share a bedroom, which might be difficult. Sharing space in the house with an extra adult will require that everyone be thoughtful and understanding. In the United States, only 40 percent of all 16- to 24-year-olds have jobs. Even people with college degrees are finding it difficult to find work.

Talking it over

Family meetings are a good way to discuss the challenges facing the family. The first concern for adults is usually money. Bills need to be paid, and coming up with a list of money-saving ideas is often a **priority**. Planning meals and only buying what is needed, using the library instead of buying books, and mending clothes instead of throwing them away are easy ways to save money. You could also offer not to receive your allowance (if you have one) for a while. By suggesting these and other ways to help out at home, such as keeping your bedroom neat or washing the dishes, you will be helping your family stay stress-free.

Talking as a family can help to share feelings and ideas for coping.

Changing places

Sometimes losing a job and **income** means losing a home. To buy a house, you usually borrow money from a bank. This is a **mortgage**, and it is paid back every month over many years. If the mortgage payments are missed, the house will be **repossessed** and the family will have to move. Repossession is when the bank takes the house back in return for the missed payments. In a similar way, if you live in a rented house and miss a rent payment, the owner may ask the family to leave.

Temporary home

If you have to move, you might live with relatives for a while. If this is not possible, you might need to find a temporary place to stay. Moving to a new home can be unsettling and make you feel sad. But it can also be an adventure and an opportunity to meet new people.

WHAT DO YOU THINK?

If your family has to move, you might not feel like talking about it. But take a look at the arguments for and against speaking up:

Keeping quiet	Speaking up
I can't change anything, so what's the point in talking?	You will feel better if you feel more involved with what's happening.
My parents are stressed enough already.	Your parents won't want you to worry about things on your own.
If I say anything, we will just argue.	Helping your parents understand how you feel can avoid arguments.

In 2008 and 2009, there were around three million homes **foreclosed** on in the United States.

New home

Sometimes families move because a parent is starting a new job. It is not always possible to move together, so your parent might go ahead to start work and the rest of the family will join him or her once a new place to stay has been arranged. Knowing that this separation is only for a short time makes it easier to cope with. Most of the time, though, families move together.

CASE STUDY

For some people, their parent's new job can mean a very big move. Isaac Parsons did not only move to a new town when his dad lost his job—he moved to a new country. When Isaac was eight, his dad got a new job in England, so the family moved over from New Zealand. "The hardest thing was leaving family and my dog behind. I was sad at the time but once we arrived it was a new adventure. I was nervous on the first day of school, but I made new friends very quickly and I had a nice teacher. I keep in touch with family and friends in New Zealand by email."

After-school activities

If you are new to your school or your parents don't have much money because of unemployment, you don't have to miss out on fun. Many schools offer clubs and activities that are held after school. These groups are usually free and are a good way of having fun, learning new skills, and making new friends.

After-school activities are a great way to have fun and make new friends.

Tough Times and Fun That's Free

What happens when parents or relatives struggle to cope with the stress of being unemployed? How do they start to look for another job? What help is out there? Your family may be going through tough times, but there are ways to cope.

Feeling low

When an adult loses his or her job, it is not only the **income** that is lost. He or she also loses work **colleagues**, daily structure, and an important sense of purpose. For some people, losing their job is like losing a loved one, and sometimes this can cause an unemployed person to become **depressed**. If this happens, doctors and **counselors** can help. In some cases, the strain of depression and unemployment can cause parental relationships to break down. You might find it hard to concentrate on your schoolwork because you are worrying about what is happening at home. Mostly, though, with family support, the depression lifts and people are able to carry on with their lives again.

It can be difficult to keep to a normal routine and stay motivated when you are unemployed and looking for another job.

Health matters

Keeping fit and healthy will help to keep the **job seeker** in a positive frame of mind and to give him or her a new routine. Walking and jogging are free activities that quickly make someone feel better. Encouraging your parent or sibling to get out and about will make them feel better about themselves and more able to look for a new job.

Lots of parks have activity trails and other fun things that you can use for free.

A positive approach

Imagine how it feels to apply for job after job only to receive **rejection** after rejection. That is the reality for many skilled, well-qualified people today. Even upbeat adults can get down and feel as though they are never going to find another job. It can be very hard to keep filling in application forms if you don't feel positive about yourself.

Are they trying?

Sometimes you might think that a parent or relative is not trying hard enough to get a new job. But are you seeing everything that the person is doing? Remember that it can be hard for an older person to find another job if his or her skills aren't **adaptable**, if he or she is sick, or if there are a lot of people applying at the same time for only a few jobs.

Coping with unemployment is stressful for everyone, and arguments sometimes happen.

To-do list and treats

Rather than getting frustrated with your parent or relative, try to help. Help draw up a job search "to-do" list. Remember to put some "fun that's free" treats in the list, too, such as visiting parks, going cycling, or having a picnic.

Showing your loved ones you care will help to keep them positive and motivated.

Online!

Keeping fit and healthy will keep your parent or relative positive. A search on the Internet will show what health facilities your town has and where they are. Most gyms are cheaper in the daytime when they are less busy, so keeping fit and feeling good doesn't have to be expensive.

Looking for support

Once you start looking, you will be amazed at how much support is out there to help unemployed people find another job. Support groups can help to stop unemployed people from feeling isolated and lonely. They also act as a very important network of contacts for future employment.

Job seeker groups

Churches, libraries, and other organizations often host groups for job seekers. These groups help people make contacts and provide support. There are online support groups, too, where people can share their experiences and feelings and get advice from people in the same situation.

Job seeker support groups meet regularly to share ideas and experiences.

Where do you find a job?

There are many places where jobs are advertised. Newspapers, magazines, online sites, and even store windows are all places that are used. You can also find job ads at a state unemployment office.

State unemployment offices

In each state, there are many state employment offices. Advisors are there to explain about **unemployment benefits** and to help people register for them. These offices have many online and paper resources to assist with job-hunting. They will also help with writing a **résumé** and filling in job application forms. All services in a state unemployment office are free and designed to help people get back to work as soon as possible.

State unemployment offices have advisors to help people match their skills to a new job.

New Beginnings

After the initial shock, having a positive attitude to the changes unemployment brings will help the whole family to get life back on track again. It might be hard to believe, but there are some positives to being unemployed, and some people actually benefit from it.

Since the start of the credit crunch, there has been a huge increase in the number of people **volunteering**. Organizations such as charities, youth clubs, sports clubs, and community projects are only able to run if they get volunteer help, and they have all benefitted from the rise in unemployment. Losing your job can result in low **self-esteem**, but helping others can be rewarding and help to increase feelings of worth. Volunteering can also provide skills and contacts that may help your parent or relative eventually find a job.

CASE STUDY

Becoming unemployed can be a surprisingly positive experience. One woman remembers how she felt when she found out she was losing her job: "At first I was mad and sad and scared. But after a while, I realized that the day I got **laid off** was the best day of my life because now I was free to do what I always wanted to do—start a craft store. For three years now I've been having so much more fun than I had in my old job. I needed the push of a layoff to get started."

Volunteering is often lots of fun and can create a new network for job searching. Here, volunteers are helping to paint a mural in a park.

It's good not to work all the time

Adults spend most of their time working, so when they aren't, it might be the first time in years that they have had some free time. They might pursue a hobby that they have always wanted to but never had time for, or decide that now is the time to work on the business idea they have had for years.

Retraining

Unemployment might also give your parent the perfect opportunity to do something different, which can lead to a better situation in the end. There are dozens of training programs offered all over the country, from plumbing and engineering to more creative art classes. Many classes are cheaper for unemployed people. Concentrating on training for a new career will help a job seeker keep a positive focus and maintain a routine.

This man is learning the skills he needs to become a plumber. Training programs may help your parent find a new career.

If your parent is unemployed, there is more time for you to have fun together.

Family time

When no one's working, family life can dramatically change in good ways, too. You might see much more of a parent who used to work long hours. Families might start doing leisure activities together, such as hiking, swimming, or cycling. Unemployment can mean that everyone takes part in family life in new and different ways.

Coping with Unemployment

Coping with changes to routine and lifestyle can be difficult for everyone in the family, but being unemployed is not the end of the world. For most people, unemployment is temporary and won't last for long. As we have seen, there are even some unexpected benefits of being unemployed. **Volunteering**, retraining, making new networks, and taking up a new hobby—all these things are positive side effects.

New job, new start

At some point, most people return to work, and life settles down into a routine once more. As we have learned, **recessions** don't last forever, and new work opportunities usually come along. In 2010, 30 weeks was the average time it took someone to find a new job after becoming unemployed. Of course, it might take longer than that or happen more quickly.

New lifestyles

Unemployment can be upsetting and difficult, but there are ways to confront it, cope with it, and move on. Your family's lifestyle might be different for a while, or you might even have to move. But no matter what the changes are, they are manageable. Keeping a routine and keeping positive will help everyone in the family cope.

No matter what your situation or experience, you are not alone. Millions of children all over the world are coping with unemployed parents, caregivers, and siblings in all kinds of different ways. If they can do it, so can you.

You will soon create your own ways to cope with unemployment and be happy.

Top Ten Tips for Coping with Unemployment

If someone in your family becomes unemployed, you might feel helpless. Here is a list of things to remember to help you and your family cope:

1. It's okay to feel sad and unhappy if your parent loses his or her job. Talking to a friend, teacher, or **counselor** will help.

2. Playing with your friends and getting some exercise is a good way to take your mind off things.

3. Doing a few household tasks to help out around the house, such as cleaning your room or washing the dishes, will be a great contribution to family life.

4. Writing things down sometimes helps you to figure out how you're feeling. Keeping a diary is a good idea.

5. Use the Internet, with adult help, to find free local fun activities that you can do with your family.

6. Suggest regular family meetings to discuss things and talk about your feelings.

7. Use your computer skills to help your parent or other relative search for jobs online.

8. Challenge your family to see who can be most creative when it comes to saving money.

9. Every evening, think of three things that made you laugh during the day and tell your family.

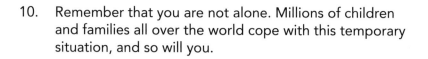

10. Remember that you are not alone. Millions of children and families all over the world cope with this temporary situation, and so will you.

It's important to have time to play, too. Friends can be great to talk to or just have fun with.

Glossary

adaptable flexible, easily adjusted

call center office equipped to handle a large amount of telephone calls from customers

colleague fellow worker

cost of living amount of money it costs to house, feed, and clothe a person or family

counselor person trained to listen to and give advice to others

crisis serious situation

depressed very unhappy

economic relating to the economy

economy system that manages money, and the production and trade of goods

efficient works well without wasting time

employee paid worker in a company or business

export ship goods overseas to be sold in other countires

financial relating to money

food aid food, or money to buy food, that is provided by the government

foreclosed house taken back by a bank due to missed mortgage payments

global economy economy of the whole world

income money earned in employment

industrialization large-scale development of businesses using machinery or computers rather than people

job fair gathering of lots of employers in one place so that unemployed people can discuss job opportunities

job seeker someone looking for a job

laid off made unemployed

manufacturing making products in factories

migrant workers workers who travel in order to find work

mortgage money borrowed to buy a house that is paid back over time

payout payment of an amount of money

priority of greater importance

protest complain, often as part of an organized group

recession period when an economy is getting worse

refinery industrial site for processing gas or oil

rejection refusal

repossessed home taken away from a buyer who has failed to keep up payments on the mortgage

restructure reorganize and change

résumé summary of someone's education and employment

seasonal only at certain times of the year, such as harvest time or Christmas

self-esteem confidence about yourself

severance pay sum of money paid by a company to a worker when he or she becomes unemployed

social networking site website that links a person with others to provide a network of contacts

supply and demand in business, how much of a product or service is available and how many people want it

unemployment benefit money given by the government to help people live while looking for a job

unpredictable unexpected, hard to foresee

volunteer work without payment

Find Out More

Books

Guillain, Charlotte. *Coping with Moving Away (Real Life Issues)*. Chicago: Heinemann Library, 2011.

Hall, Margaret. *Money (Earning, Saving, Spending)*. Chicago: Heinemann Library, 2008.

Lynette, Rachel. *What to Do When Your Parent Is Out of Work (Let's Work It Out)*. New York: PowerKids, 2010.

Orr, Tamra. *Money Matters: A Kid's Guide to Money*. Hockessin, Del.: Mitchell Lane, 2009.

Weissmann, Joe. *Can I Catch It Like a Cold? Coping with a Parent's Depression*. Toronto: Tundra, 2009.

Websites and organizations

The following websites and organizations can offer help and support to you and your family:

Big Brothers Big Sisters
www.bbbsi.org
Big Brothers Big Sisters is a mentoring organization that helps children from 6 to 18 years old. Children are given a mentor to support them and help them through difficult times.

Kids' Health: What Kids Who Are Moving Should Do
http://kidshealth.org/kid/feeling/home_family/moving.html
Kids' Health offers lots of helpful tips and ideas for kids
who are moving.

Kids' Money
www.kidsmoney.org/kids.htm
Visit this website to find out money-saving tips to make your
pocket money go further and help you save for the future.

Free activities

Free activities in your area can be found by asking at visitor
centers, libraries, or going online and searching for "Free
activities in [name of your town]" and put in your town or
the nearest large city. Remember to ask an adult to help you
when you use the Internet. If you're moving to a new town, try
searching online to find out what facilities the town has to offer.

Index